George Laurence Gomme

The History of Thomas Hickathrift

Printed from the earliest extant copies

George Laurence Gomme

The History of Thomas Hickathrift
Printed from the earliest extant copies

ISBN/EAN: 9783337251383

Printed in Europe, USA, Canada, Australia, Japan

Cover: Foto ©ninafisch / pixelio.de

More available books at **www.hansebooks.com**

THE HISTORY

OF

THOMAS HICKATHRIFT.

PRINTED FROM

THE EARLIEST EXTANT COPIES.

AND EDITED, WITH AN INTRODUCTION,

BY

GEORGE LAURENCE GOMME, F.S.A.

LONDON:

PRINTED FOR THE VILLON SOCIETY.

1885.

Introduction.

THERE seems to be some considerable reason for believing that the hero of this story was a reality. The story tells us that he lived in the marsh of the Isle of Ely, and that he became "a brewer's man" at Lyn, and traded to Wisbeach. This little piece of geographical evidence enables us to fix the story as belonging to the great Fen District, which occupied the north of Cambridgeshire and Norfolk.

The antiquary Thomas Hearne has gone so far as to identify the hero of tradition with a doughty knight of the Crusaders. Writing in the *Quarterly Review* (vol. xxi. p. 102), Sir Francis Palgrave says :—

" Mr. Thomas Hickathrift, afterwards Sir Thomas Hickathrift, Knight, is praised by Mr. Thomas Hearne as a ' famous champion.' The honest antiquary has identified this well-known knight with the far less celebrated Sir Frederick de Tylney, Baron of Tylney in Norfolk, the ancestor of the Tylney family, who was killed at Acon, in Syria, in the reign of Richard Cœur de Lion. Hycophric, or Hycothrift, as the mister-wight observes, being probably a corruption of Frederick.

This happy exertion of etymological acumen is not wholly due to Hearne, who only adopted a hint given by Mr. Philip le Neve, whilome of the College of Arms."

There does not seem to be the slightest evidence for Hearne's identification any more than there is for his philological conclusions, and we may pass over this for other and more reliable information.

We must first of all turn to the story itself, as it has come down to us in its chapbook form. It is divided into two parts. The first part of the story is the earliest; the second part being evidently a printer's or a chapman's addition. Our reprint of the former is taken from the copy in the Pepysian Library at Magdalene College, Cambridge, and which was printed probably about 1660—1690; the latter is taken from the British Museum copy, the date of which, according to the Museum authorities, is 1780.

In trying to ascertain something as to the date of the story apart from that of its printed version, it will therefore be necessary to put out of consideration the second portion. This has been written by some one well acquainted with the original first part, and with the spirit of the story; but in spite of this there is undoubted evidence of its literary origin at a date later than the first part. But turning to the first part there are two expressions in this early Pepysian version which have not been repeated in the later editions—those of the eighteenth century; and these two expressions appear to me to indicate a date *after which* the story could not have been originated.   On page 1 we read that Tom Hickathrift dwelt " in the *marsh* of the Isle of Ely."   In the earliest Brit'sh Museum copy this appears as "in the *parish* of the Isle of Ely."   Again, on page 11 Tom is described as laying out the giant's estate, "some of which he gave to the poor for their common, and the rest he made pastures of and divided the most part into *good ground*, to maintain him and his old mother Jane Hickathrift."   In the earliest British Museum copy the expression " good ground " is displaced by " tillage."   Now it is clear from these curious transposition of words in the earliest and latest editions that something had been going on to change the nature of the country. The eighteenth-century people did not know the " marsh " of Ely, so they read " parish ": they did not know the meaning of " good ground " so they read " tillage."   And hence it is clear that at the printing of this earliest version the fen lands of Cambridge and Norfolk had not yet been drained ; there was still " marsh land " which was being made into " good land."

But I think there is evidence in this printed chap-book version of the story which tells us that it was taken from a traditional version.   Let any one take the trouble to read aloud the first part, and he will at once perceive that there is a ring and a cadence given to the voice by the wording of the story, and particularly by the curious punctuation, which at once reminds us of a narrative from word of mouth.   And besides this there is some little evidence of phonetic spelling, just such as might have been expected from the first printer taking the story from the lips of one of the Fen-country peasantry.

Now this internal evidence of the once *viva-voce* existence of the printed legend of Tom Hickathrift has a direct bearing upon the question as to the date of the earliest printed version. The colloquialisms are so few, and the rhythm, though marked and definite, is occasionally so halting and approaches so nearly a literary form, that we are forced to observe that the earliest printed edition now known is certainly not the earliest version printed. There are too few phoneticisms and dialect words to make it probable that the print in the Pepysian collection is the one directly derived from popular tradition. As the various printers in the eighteenth century altered words and sentences here and there, as different editions were issued, so did the seventeenth-century printers; and therefore it is necessary to push the date of the printed version farther back than we can hope to ascertain by direct evidence. There is no reason why there should not have been a sixteenth-century printed version, and to this period I am inclined to allocate the earliest appearance of the story in print.

And then prior to the printed version was the popular version with its almost endless life, perhaps reaching back to that vague period indicated in the opening words of the story, " in the reign before William the Conqueror." Already internal evidence has, it is suggested, pointed to a popular unwritten tradition of Tom Hickathrift's life and exploits. But we must

ask now, Is there, or was there, any tradition among the peasantry of Lyn and its neighbourhood about Thomas Hickathrift? And, if so, how far does this popular tradition reach
back, and how far does it tally with the chap-book version?
Again, is this popular tradition independent of the chap-book
story, or has it been generated from the printed book? To
answer these questions properly we must closely examine all
the evidence available as to the existence and form of this
popular tradition.

Turning first of all to the historian of Norfolk, Blomefield,*
writing in 1808, gives us the following account :—

"The town of Tilney gives name to a famous common
called Tilney Smeeth, whereon 30,000 or more large Marshland sheep and the great cattle of seven towns to which it
belongs are constantly said to feed. Of this plain of Smeeth
there is a tradition, *which the common people retain,* that in
old time the inhabitants of these towns [Tilney, Terrington,
Clenchwarton, Islington, Walpole, West Walton, Walsoken,
and Emneth] had a contest with the lords of the manors about
the bounds and limits of it, when one *Hickifric,* a person of
great stature and courage, assisting the said inhabitants in their
rights of common, took an axle-tree from a cart-wheel, instead

---

* Blomefield's *History of Norfolk,* vol. ix. pp. 79-80; the same story is related by
Chambers in his *History of Norfolk,* vol. i. p. 370. The parishes of W. and N. Lynn,
though lying in marshland, are excluded from any right of pasturage on the Smeeth
Common.

b

of a sword, and the wheel for a shield or buckler, and thus armed
soon repelled the invaders. And for proof of this notable exploit
they to this day show, says Sir William Dugdale [Dugd. *Hist. of
Imbanking*, &c. p. 244 ; Weever's *Fun. Mon.* p. 866], a large
grave-stone near the east end of the chancel in Tilney churchyard, whereon the form of a cross is so cut or carved as that
the upper part thereof (wherewith the carver hath adorned it)
being circular, they will therefore needs have it to be the grave-
stone of *Hickifric*, and to be as a memorial of his gallantry.
The stone coffin, which stands now out of the ground in
Tilney churchyard, on the north side of the church, will not
receive a person above six feet in length, and this is shown as
belonging formerly to the giant *Hickifric*. The cross said to
be a representation of the cart-wheel is a cross pattée, on the
summit of a staff, which staff is styled an axle-tree. Such crosses
pattée on the head of a staff were emblems or tokens that some
Knight Templar was therein interred, and many such are to be
seen at this day in old churches."

Now the reference to Sir William Dugdale is misleading,
because, as will be seen by the following quotation, the position
of the hero is altered in Dugdale's version of the legend from
that of a popular leader to the tyrant lord himself:—" Of this
plain I may not omit a tradition which the common people
thereabouts have, viz., that in old time the inhabitants of the
neighbouring villages had a fierce contest with one Hickifric
(the then owner of it) touching the bounds thereof, which

grew so hot that at length it came to blows; and that Hickifric, being a person of extraordinary stature and courage, took
an axletree from a cart instead of a sword, and the wheel for
his buckler, and, being so armed, most stoutly repelled those bold
invaders: for further testimony of which notable exploit they
to this day show a large gravestone near the east end of the
chancel in Tilney churchyard, whereupon the form of a cross
is so cut as that the upper part thereof by reason of the flou-
rishes (wherewith the carver hath adorned it) sheweth to
be somewhat circular, which they will, therefore, needs have
to be the wheel and the shaft the axletree." This version,
taken from Dugdale's *History of Imbanking*, 1772, p. 244,
though differing in form, at all events serves to carry us back
to 1662, the date when Sir William Dugdale's *History* was first
published.

But the local tradition can be carried further back than
1662, because the learned Sir Henry Spelman, in his *Icenia
sive Norfolciae Descriptio Topographica*, p. 138, and written
about 1640, says, when speaking of Tilney, in Marshland
Hundred: "Hic se expandit insignis area quæ à planicie nun-
cupatur Tylney-smelth, pinguis adeo et luxurians ut Paduana
pascua videatur superasse. . . . . Tuentur eam indigenæ velut
Aras et Focos, fabellamque recitant longa petitam vetustate
de Hikifrico (nescio quo) Haii illius instar in Scotorum
Chronicis, qui Civium suorum dedignatus fuga, Aratrum
quod agebat, solvit; arreptoque Temone furibundus insiliit

in hostes victoriamque ademit exultantibus. Sic cum de agri
istius finibus acriter olim dimicatum esset inter fundi Dominun
et Villarum Incolas, nec valerent hi adversus eum consistere;
redeuntibus occurrit Hikifricus, axemque excutiens a curru
quem agebat, eo vice Gladii usus; Rotâ, Clypei; invasores
repulit ad ipsos quibus nunc funguntur terminos. Ostendunt
in cæmeterio Tilniensi, Sepulcrum sui pugilis, Axem cum
Rota insculptum exhibens.''

A still earlier version is to be found recorded by Weever
in 1631. The full quotation is as follows : " Tylney Smeeth,
so called of a smooth plaine or common thereunto adioyning.
. . . In the Churchyard is a ridg'd Altar, Tombe, or sepulchre
of a wondrous antique fashion, vpon which an axell-tree and
a cart wheele are insculped. Vnder this Funerall Monument
the Towne dwellers say that one Hikifricke lies interred; of
whom *(as it hath gone by tradition from father to the sonne)*
they thus likewise report : How that vpon a time (no man
knowes how long since) there happened a great quarrell betwixt
the Lord of this land or ground and the inhabitants of the
foresaid seuen villages, about the meere-marks, limits, or bon-
daries of this fruitfull feeding place; the matter came to a
battell or skirmish, in which the said Inhabitants being not
able to resist the landlord and his forces began to giue backe;
Hikifricke, driuing his cart along and perceiuing that his
neighbours were fainthearted, and ready to take flight, he
shooke the Axell tree from the cart which he vsed instead of a

sword, and tooke one of the cart-wheeles which he held as a buckler; with these weapons he set vpon the Common aduersaries or aduersaries of the Common, encouraged his neighbours to go forward, and fight valiantly in defence of their liberties; who being animated by his manly prowesse, they tooke heart to grasse, as the prouerbe is, insomuch that they chased the Landlord and his companie to the vtmost verge of the said Common; which from that time they haue quietly enioyed to this very day. The Axell-tree and cart-wheele are cut and figured in diuers places of the Church and Church windowes, which makes the story, you must needs say, more probable. This relation doth in many parts parallell with that of one Hay, a strong braue spirited Scottish Plowman, who vpon a set battell of Scots against the Danes, being working at the same time in the next field, and seeing some of his countreymen to flie from that hote encounter, caught vp an oxe yoke (Boëthius saith, a Plough-beame), with which (after some exhortation that they should not bee fainthearted) he beate the said straglers backe againe to the maine Army, where he with his two sonnes (who tooke likewise such weapons as came next to their hands) renewed the charge so furiously that they quite discomfited the enemy, obtaining the glory of the day and victory for their drad Lord and Soueraigne Kenneth the third, King of Scotland; and this happened in the yeare 942, the second of the King's raigne. This you may reade at large in the *History of Scotland*, thus abridged

by Camden as followeth."—Weever's *Funerall Monuments,*
1631, pp. 866-867.

And Sir Francis Palgrave, quoting the legend from Spelman,
observes,—"From the most remote antiquity the fables and
achievements of Hickifric have been obstinately credited by the
inhabitants of the township of Tylney. Hickifric is venerated
by them as the assertor of the rights and liberties of their an-
cestors. The 'monstrous giant' who guarded the marsh was
in truth no other than the tyrannical lord of the manor who
attempted to keep his copyholders out of the common field,
Tylney Smeeth; but who was driven away with his retainers
by the prowess of Tom armed only with his axletree and
cart-wheel."* This does not appear to me to put the case too
strongly. A tradition told so readily and believed so generally
in the middle of the seventeenth century must have had a
strong vitality in it only to be obtained by age.

Let us now turn to the other side, namely, the existence of
a traditional version in modern days, because it is important
to note that the printing of a chapbook version need not have
disturbed the full current of traditional thought. In a note Sir
Francis Palgrave seems to imply that the story was still extant
without the aid of printed literature. He writes :

"A Norfolk antiquary has had the goodness to procure for
us an authentic report of the present state of Tom's sepulchre.

* *Quarterly Review,* vol. xxi. p. 103.

It is a stone soros, of the usual shape and dimensions; the sculptured lid or cover no longer exists. It must have been entire about fifty years ago, for when we were good *Gaffer Crane would rehearse Tom's achievements*, and tell us that he had cut out the moss which filled up the inscription with his penknife, but he could not read the letters." *

And Clare, in his *Village Minstrel*, tells us that:—

" Here Lubin listen'd with awestruck surprise,
    When Hickathrift's great strength has met his ear;
    How he kil'd giants as they were but flies,
    And lifted trees as one would a spear,
    Though not much bigger than his fellows were;
    He knew no troubles waggoners have known,
    Of getting stall'd and such disasters drear;
    Up he'd chuck sacks as we would hurl a stone,
    And draw whole loads of grain unaided and alone."

And this view as to the existence still of a traditional form of the story is almost borne out by what the country people only recently had to say relative to a monument in that part of the country over which Sir William Dugdale travelled, and of which he has left us such a valuable memorial in his *History of Imbanking*. A writer in the Journal of the Archæological Association (vol. xxv. p. 11) says:—"A mound close to the Smeeth Road Station, between Lynn and Wisbech, is called the Giant's

* *Quarterly Review,* vol. xxi. p. 102, note.

Grave, and the inhabitants relate that there lie the remains of
the great giant slain by Hickathrift with the cart wheel and
axletree. A cross was erected upon it, and is to be seen in the
neighbouring churchyard of Torrington St. John's, bearing the
singular name of Hickathrift's Candlestick."

It appears, then, that the following may be considered the
chief evidence which we have obtained about the existence of
the story :—

> That a chapbook or literary form of the story has existed
>   from the sixteenth century ;
> That a traditional story existed quite independently of the
>   literary story in the seventeenth century ;
> That a traditional story exists at the present time, or until
>   very recently ;

And knowing what folk-lore has to say about the long life of
traditions, about their constant repetition age after age, it is not,
I venture to think, too much to conclude that a story which
can be shown by evidence to have lived on from mouth to
mouth for two centuries is capable of going back to an almost
endless antiquity for its true original.

Let us now consider what may be the origin of this story.
There is one theory as to this which has gained the authority
of Sir Francis Palgrave. The pranks which Tom performed
" must be noticed," says Sir Francis, " as being correctly Scandinavian " He then goes on to say, " Similar were the achievements of the great Northern champion Grettir, when he kept

geese upon the common, as told in his Saga. Tom's youth retraces the tales of the prowess of the youthful Siegfried detailed in the Niblunga Saga and in the book of Heroes. It appears from Hearne that the supposed axle-tree, with the superincumbent wheel, was represented on 'Hycothrift's' grave-stone in Tylney churchyard in the shape of a cross. This is the form in which all the Runic monuments represent the celebrated hammer or thunderbolt of the son of Odin, which shattered the skulls and scattered the brains of so many luckless giants. How far this surmise may be supported by Tom's skill and strength in throwing the hammer we will not pretend to decide." *

Now this takes the story entirely out of the simple category of local English tradition, and places it at once among those grand mythic tales which belong to the study of comparative mythology and which take us back to the earliest of man's thought and belief. In order to test this theory let us have before us the passages in Tom Hickathrift's history which might be said to bear it out, and then let us compare them with the stories of Grettir.

The analysis of the story based upon the plan laid down by the Folk-Lore Society is as follows :—

(1.) Tom's parents are nobodies, "a poor man and day labourer" being his father.

---

* *Quarterly Review,* vol. xxi. pp. 102-103.

(2.) Tom was obstinate as a boy.

(3.) Loses his father, and at first does not help his mother, but sits in the chimney corner.

(4.) Is of great height and size.

(5.) Strength is unknown until he shows it.

(6.) Commits many pranks, among which is the throwing "a hammer five or six furlongs off into a river."

(7.) Kills a giant with a club, Tom using axletree and wheel for his shield and buckler.

(8.) Takes possession of the giant's territory and lives there.

(9.) Commits more pranks, "kicks a football right away."

(10.) Escapes from four thieves and despoils them.

(11.) Is defeated by a tinker.

It will not be necessary to analyse the whole of the stories to which we are referred for the mythic parallels of Tom Hickka-thrift; but I will take out the items corresponding to those tabulated above. In the story of "Grettir the Strong" we have the following incidents :—

(1.) Grettir's father "had his homestead and farm land."

(2.) Grettir was obstinate as a boy (does nothing on board ship.)

(3.) Plays pranks upon his father, and returns from attending the horses to the fire-side (Iceland).

(4.) Is short, though strong, and big of body.

(5.) He had not skill to turn his great strength to account.

(6.) He wrestles with other lads, and commits many
    pranks, flings a rock from its place.
(7.) Wrestles with Karr, the barrow dweller; and
(8.) Takes possession of Karr's weapons and wealth.
(9.) Fights with and conquers robbers.

Now it cannot be denied that there is a great similarity in
the thread of these two stories. Norfolk, the colony of the
Northmen of old, may well have retained its ancient tradition
until the moving incidents of English economic history brought
about the weaving of it into the actual life that was pressing
round men's thoughts. It would thus leave out the great mass
of detail in the old northern tradition, and retain just sufficient
to fit in with the new requirements; and in this way it appears
to me we have the present form of the story of Tom Hickathrift, its ancient Scandinavian outline, its more modern English
application. Now it is curious to note that the cart-wheel
plays a not unimportant part in English folk-lore as a repre-
sentative of old runic faith. Sir Henry Ellis, in his edition of
Brand's *Popular Antiquities* (vol. i. p. 298), has collected together some instances of this; and whatever causes may have led
to this survival there is nothing to prevent us from looking
upon the wheel and axle in the story of Tom Hickathrift as a
part and parcel of the same survival.

There now remains to notice one or two points of interest
outside the narrative of the story itself. Of curious expressions
we have—

fitted (p. 3), to pay any one out, to revenge one's self;

buttle of straw (p. 3);

shift (p. 3), to support, to make shift. See Davies's *Supplementary Glossary, sub voce* "make-shift," "shiftful";

bone-fires (p. 11). See Ellis's *Brand's Popular Antiquities,* vol. i. p. 300, note;

cocksure (p. 14), quite sure.

Of proverbs there are—

to win the horse or lose the saddle (p. 8);

to make hay while the sun did shine (p. 10).

Of games there are mentioned—

cudgells (p. 4);

wrestling (p. 4);

throwing the hammer (p. 4);

football (p. 13);

bear-baiting (p. 13).

It will be observed that the spelling of the name in the Pepysian copy is specially divided thus — Hic - ka - thrift; and though it seems probable that some good reason must be assigned to this, I cannot find out points of importance. But about the dubbing him Mr. (p. 7) or Master, as it would be in full, there is something of great interest to point out. This was formerly a distinct title. In Harrison's *Description of England* we read, "Who soeuer studieth the lawes of the realme, who so abideth in the vniuersitie, or professeth physicke and the liberall sciences, or beside his seruice in the roome of a capteine in the warres can liue without manuell labour, and thereto is able and will beare the post, charge, and countenance of a gentleman, he shall be called master, which is the title that men giue to esquiers and gentlemen and reputed for gentlemen."—Harrison's *Description of England,* 1577 (edited by F. J. Furnivall for the New Shakspere Society, 1877), p. 129.

Of yeomen he says, " And albeit they be not called master as gentlemen are, or sir as to knights apperteineth, but onelie John and Thomas," &c. (p. 134): and of " the third and last sort," " named the yeomanrie," he adds, " that they be not called masters and gentlemen, but goodmen, as goodman Smith, goodman Coot, goodman Cornell, goodman Mascall, goodman Cockswet," &c. (p. 137).

Mr. Furnivall's note (p. 123) is as follows :—"*Every Begger almost is called Maister.*—See Lancelot's ' MAISTER Launcelet ' in the *Merchant of Venice,* II. ii. 51, and the extract illustrating it from Sir Thomas Smith's *Commonwealth of England,* bk. I. ch. 20 (founded on Harrison, i. 133, 137), which I printed in *New Sh. Soc.'s Trans.* 1877-9, p. 103-4. Also Shakspere getting his ' yeoman ' father arms, and making him a ' gentleman ' in 1596.—(Leopold Shakspere, Introduction, p. ciii.)." We thus get still further indication of the early date of the story, the significance of the title "Master" having died out during the seventeenth century.

The following is a bibliographical list of some of the editions,

many others having been printed from the beginning of this
century:—

    (1.) The history of Thomas Hickathrift. Printed for the
    booksellers. London [1790.] 12mo. pp. 24.

      Cap. i. Of his birth, parentage, and education. ii.
    How Thomas Hickathrift's strength came to be
    known. iii. How Tom came to be a Brewer's man;
    and how he came to kill a giant, and at last was
    Mr. Hickathrift. iv. How Tom kept a pack of hounds;
    his kicking a football quite away; also how he had like
    to have been robbed by four thieves, and how he escaped.

    (2.) The Pleasant and delightful history of Thomas Hicka-
    thrift. Whitehaven: printed by Ann Dunn, Market
    Place [1780], pp. 24.

    (3.) The History of Thomas Hickathrift. Printed in
    Aldermary Churchyard, London. [1790.] 12mo. Part
    the first, pp. 24.

      Similar contents to No. 1, with addition of cap. v.
    Tom meets with a Tinker, and of the battle they fought.

    (4.) The most pleasant and delightful history of Thomas
    Hickathrift. J. Terraby, printer, Market Place, Hull.
    [1825.] 2 parts. 12mo. pp. 24; 24.

      Same as No. 1. Second part, cap. i. How Tom
    Hickathrift and the Tinker conquered ten thousand
    rebels. ii. How Tom Hickathrift and the Tinker were
    sent for up to court, and of their kind entertainment.

iii. How Tom, after his mother's death, went a-wooing, and of the trick he served a gallant who affronted him. iv. How Tom served two troopers whom this spark had hired to beset him. v. Tom, going to be married, was set upon by one and twenty ruffians, and the havock he made. vi. Tom made a feast for all the poor widows in the adjacent houses, and how he served an old woman who stole a silver cup at the same time. vii. How Sir Thomas Hickathrift and his lady were sent for up to court, and of what happened at that time. viii. How Tom was made Governor of the East Angles, now called Thanet, and of the wonderful achievement he performed there. ix. How the Tinker, hearing of Tom's fame, went to be his partner, and how he was unfortunately slain by a lion.

(5.) The history of Thomas Hickathrift. Printed for the Travelling Stationers. 12mo. pp. 24.

Same as No. 3.

THE

PLEASANT HISTORY

OF

THOMAS HIC-KA-THRIFT.

Printed by J. M. for W. Thackeray and T. Passinger.

THE

CONTENTS.

THE

PLEASANT HISTORY

OF

THOMAS HIC-KA-THRIFT,

His Birth and Parentage, and the true man-
ner of his performing many manly acts,
and how he killed a gyant.
Young man, here thou mayest behold what
honour Tom came unto.

And if that thou dost buy this Book,
Be sure that thou dost in it look,
And read it o're, then thou wilt say,
Thy money is not thrown away.

In the reign before William the conqueror, I have read in ancient histories that there dwelt a man in the marsh of the Isle of Ely, in the county of Cambridge, whose name was Thomas Hic-ka-thrift, a poor man and day labourer, yet he was a very stout man, and able to perform two days works instead of one: He having one son and no more children in the world, he called him by his own name, Thomas Hickathrift. This old man put his son to good learning, but he would take none, for he was as we call them now in this age, none of the wisest sort, but something soft, and had no docility at all in him.

God calling this old man his father out of the world, his mother being tender of him, and maintained him by her hand labour as well as she could; he being sloathful and not willing to work to get a penny for his living, but all his delight was to be in the chimney corner, and would eat as much at one time as might very well serve four or five ordinary men; for he was in length when he was but ten years of age about eight foot, and in thickness five foot, and his hand was like unto a shoulder of mutton, and in all parts from top to toe he was like a monster, and yet his great strength was not known.

How Tom Hic-ka-thrifts strength came to be known, the which if you please but to read will give you full satisfaction.

The first time that his strength was known was by his mothers going to a rich farmer's house (she being but a poor woman) to desire a buttle of straw to shift herself and her son Thomas. The farmer being an honest charitable man, bid her take what she would. She going home to her son Tom, said, I pray thee go to such a place and fetch me a buttle of straw, I have asked him leave. He swore a great oath he would not go: nay, prithee, Tom go, said his old mother. He swore again he would not go, unless she would borrow him a cart rope. She being willing to please him, because she would have some straw, went and borrowed him a cart rope to his desire.

He taking it went his way; so coming to the farmer's house, the master was in the barn, and two men a thrashing. Said Tom, I am come for a buttle of straw. Tom, said the master, take as much as thou canst carry. He laid down his cart rope, and began to make his buttle; but said they, Tom, thy rope is to short, and jeer'd poor Tom, but he fitted the man well for it : for he made his buttle, and when he had made it, there was supposed to be a load of straw in it, of two thousand weight. But said they, what a great fool art thou, thou canst not carry the tith on't ? but Tom took the buttle and flung it on his shoulder, and made no more of it then we do of an hundred weight, to the great admiration of master and men.

Tom Hic-ka-thrift's strength being known in the town, then they would not let him any longer lie basking by the fire in the chimney corner, every one would be hiring him to work ; they seeing him to have so much strength, told him that it was a shame for him to live such a lazy course of life, and to lie idle day after day, as he did. So Tom seeing them bait at him in such a manner as they did, he went first to one work then to another ; but at length came a man to Tom and desired him to go with him unto the wood, for he had a tree to bring home, and he would content him. So Tom went with him, and he took with him four men beside ; but when they came to the wood, they set the cart by the tree and began to draw it up with pullies ; but Tom seeing them not able to lift it up, said, stand away, you fools, and takes the tree and sets it on one end, a nd lays it in the cart. Now, says he, see what a man can do. Marry, it is true, said they. So when they had done coming through the wood they met the woodman, Tom asked him for a stick to make his mother a fire with. I, said the wood-man, take one what thou canst carry. So Tom espyed a tree bigger then was in the cart, and lays it on his shoulder, and goes home

with it as fast as the cart and six horses could draw it. This
was the second time that Tom's strength was known.

So when Tom began to know that he had more strength
then twenty men had, he then began to be merry with men
and very tractable, and would run, or go, or jump, and took
great delight to be amongst company, and to go to fairs and
meetings, and to see sports and pastimes. So going to a feast,
the young men were all met, some to cudgels, some to wrastling.
some throwing the hammer, and the like; so Tom stood a
little to see their sport, and at last goes to them that were a
throwing the hammer; and standing a little by to behold their
manlike sport, at last he takes the hammer in his hand to feel
the weight of it, and bid them stand out of the way, for he
would throw it as far as he could. I, said the smith, and jeer'd
poor Tom, you'l threw it a great way I'le warrant you; but
Tom took the hammer and flung it; and there was a river
about five or six furlungs off, and flung it into that: so when
he had done, he bid the smith go fetch his hammer again, and
laught the smith to scorn; but when Tom had done that, he
would go to wrastling, though he had no more skill than an
ass had, but what he did by strength; yet he flung all that
came, for if once he laid hold they were gone. Some he would
throw over his head, some he would lay down slyly, and how
he pleased; he would not lock nor strike at their heels, but
flung them two or three yards from him, ready to break their
necks asunder; so that none at last durst go into the ring to

B

wrastle with him, for they took him to be some devil that was come amongst them ; so Tom's fame was spread more in the country.

How Tom came to be a Brewer's man; and how he came to kill a Giant, and at last was Mr. Hic-ka-thrift.

Tom's fame being spread abroad in the country, there was not a man durst give Tom an angry word for he was something foolhardy, and he did not care what he did at them; so that those that knew him would not in the least displease him. But at length there was a brewer at Lyn, that wanted a good lusty man to carry his beer in the marsh and to Wisbech; so hearing of Tom went to hire him, but Tom seemed coy and would not be his man, until his mother and friends did perswade him, and his master intreated him; and likewise promised him a new suit of clothes and cloath him from top to toe; and besides he should eat and drink of the best. So Tom at last yielded to be his man, and his master told him how far he should go; for you are to understand there was a monstrous Gyant, who kept some part of the marsh, and none durst go that way; for if they did he would keep them or kill them, or else he would make bond slaves of them.

But to come to Tom and his master, that he did more work

in one day then all his men would do in three; so that his master, seeing him so tractable, and to look so well after his business, made him his head man to go into the marsh, to carry beer by himself, for he needed no man with him. So Tom went every day to Wisbich, which was a very great journey, for it was twenty mile the road way.

Tom going so long that wearisome journey, and finding that way which the Gyant kept was nearer by half, and Tom having gotten more strength by half then before by being so well kept, and drinking so much strong ale as he did; one day he was going to Wisbich, and without saying anything to his master or to any of his fellow servants, he was resolved to make the nearest way to be a road or lose his life, to win the horse, or lose the saddle; to kill or be killed; if he met with the Gyant; and with this resolution he goes the nearest way with his cart, flinging open the gates for his cart and horses to go through; but at last the Gyant spying him, and seeing him to be so bold, thought to prevent him, and came intending to take his beer for a prize, but Tom cared not a fart for him, and the Gyant he met Tom like a lyon, as though he would have swallowed him. Sirrah, said he, who gave you authority to come this way? Do you not know that I make all stand in fear of my sight, and you like a rogue must come and fling my gates open at your pleasure! How dare you presume to do this? Are you so careless of your life? Do you not care what you do? I'le make thee an example for all rogues under the sun; dost thou not see how many heads hang upon yonder tree that have offended my law! But thy head shall hang higher then all the rest for an example. But Tom made him answer, A turd in your teeth for your news, for you shall not find me like one of them. No, said the Gyant, why thou art but a fool, dost thou come to fight with such a one as I am, and bring no weapon to defend 'thyself withal? Said Tom, I have a weapon here will make you to know you are a traytorly rogue. I, sirrah, said the Gyant, and took that word in high disdain, that Tom should call him a traytorly rogue, and with that he ran into his cave to fetch his great club, intending to dash out Tom's brains at the first blow.

Tom knew not what to do for a weapon, for he knew his whip would do but little good against such a monstrous beast as he was, for he was in length twelve foot, and six foot about the waste; but while the Gyant went for his club, Tom bethought himself of a very good weapon, for he makes no more ado, but takes his cart and turns it upside down, and takes the axletree and the wheel for his shield and buckler, and very good weapons they were in such time of need.

The Giant coming out again, began to stare at Tom, to see him take the wheel in one hand and the axle tree in the other to defend himself with. O! said the Gyant, you are like to do great service with those weapons; I have here a twig, said the Gyant, that will beat thee and thy wheel and axle tree at once unto the ground; that which the Gyant called a twig was as thick as some mill posts are, but Tom was not daunted for all that, for he saw there was but one way to kill or be killed; so the Giant made at Tom with such a vehement force that he made Tom's wheel crack again, and Tom lent the Gyant another as good, for he took him such a weighty blow on the side of the head that he made the Gyant reel again. What, said Tom, are you drunk with my strong beer already.   •

The Gyant recovering laid on Tom most sad blows; but still as they came Tom kept them off with his wheel so that he had no hurt at all. Tom plyed his work so well, and laid such huge blows at the Giant, that the sweat and blood together ran down his face, and he being fat and foggy, and fighting so long, was almost tired out, asked Tom to let him drink a little, and then he would fight with him again. No, said Tom, my mother did not teach me that wit ; whose a fool then ? Tom seeing the Gyant begin to be weary, and finding him to fail in his blows, he thought best to make hay while the sun did shine, for he laid on so fast as though he had been mad, till he had brought the Gyant to the ground. The Gyant seeing himself down, and Tom laying so hard on him, roared in a most sad condition, and prayed him not to take away his life and he would do anything for him, and yield himself to him and be his servant ; but Tom having no more mercy on him then a dog of a bear, laid still at the Gyant 'till he had laid him for dead, and when he had done he cut off his head and went into his cave, and there he found great store of silver and gold which made his heart to leap. But when he had done, he loaded his cart and went to Wisbich and delivered his beer; and coming home to his master, he told it to him; but his master was so overjoy'd at the news that he would not believe him till he had seen; and getting up the next day he and his master went to see if he spoke true or no, and most of the town of Lyn. But when they came to the place and found the Gyant dead, he shewed them where the head was, and what silver and gold there was in the cave, all of them leapt for joy, for the Gyant was a great enemy to all the country.

This news was spread all up and down the country how Tom Hic-ka-thrift had kill'd the Gyant, and well was he that could run or go to see the Gyant and the cave; then all the folks made bonefires for joy; and Tom was a better man respected then before. · And Tom took possession of the cave by consent of the country, and everyone said that he did deserve twice as much more. So Tom pulled down the cave and built him a brave house where the cave stood; all the ground that the Gyant kept by force and strength, some he gave to the poor for their common, and the rest he made pastures of and divided the most part into good ground to maintain him and his old mother Jane Hic-ka-thrift. And Tom's fame was spread both far and near throughout the country; and then it was no longer Tom, but Mr. Hickathrift, so that he was now the chiefest man amongst them, for the people feared Tom's anger as much as they did the Gyant before. So Tom kept men

and maids, and lived most bravely ; and he made him a park to
keep deer in ; and by his house, which is a town, he built a
famous church and gave it the name of St. James' Church,
because he killed the Gyant on that day, which is so to this
hour and ever will be; and many more good deeds he did which
is too tedious to write in this column, but to tell the chief I
shall do my endeavour.

How Tom kept a pack of Hounds; and kickt a Foot-ball quite away; and how he had like to have been robbed by Four Thieves, and how he escaped.

Tom having so much about him and not used to it could hardly tell how for to dispose of it, but yet he did use a means to do it, for he kept a pack of hounds, and men to hunt with him; and who but Tom then. So he took such delight in sport that he would go far and near to any meetings, as cudgel-play, bear-baiting, football play, and the like. But as Tom was riding one day, he seeing a company at football play he lighted off his horse to see that rare sport, for they were playing for a wager; but Tom was a stranger there and none did know him there; but Tom soon spoiled their sport, for he meeting the football took it such a kick that they never found their ball no more; they could see it fly, but whither none could tell, nor to what place; they all wondered at it, and began to quarrel with Tom, but some of them got nothing by it, for Tom gets a spar which belonged to a house that was blown down and all that stood in his way he either killed or knocked down, so that all the country was up in arms to take Tom, but all in vain, for he

c

manfully made way wherever he came. So when he was gone from them, and was going homeward, he chanced to be somewhat late in the evening. On the road there met him four lusty rogues that had been robbing of passengers that way, and none could escape them, for they robbed all they met, both rich and poor. They thought when they met Tom they should get a good prize, they perceiving he was alone, made them cocksure of his money, but they were mistaken, for he got a prize by them. When they met with Tom they straight bid him stand and deliver. What, said Tom, what should I deliver? Your money, sirrah, said they. But, said Tom, you shall give me better words for it first, and be better armed too. Come, come, said they, we do not come hither to prate, but we come for money, and money we will have before you stir from this place. I, said Tom, is it so? Nay then, said he, get it, and take it.

So one of them made at him, but he presently unarmed him, and took away his sword which was made of good trusty steel, and smote so hard at the others that they began to set spurs to their horses and begone, but he soon stayed their journey, one of them having a portmantle behind him, Tom perceiving it to be money fought with more courage then he did before, till at the last he had killed two of the four, and the other two he wounded most grievously that they cryed for quarter. So with much intreating he gave them quarter, but he took all their money which was two hundred pounds to bear his charges home. So when Tom came home he told them how he had served the football players and the four thieves which caused a laugh from his old mother, and to refresh himself went to see how all things did, and what his men had done since he went from home. And going to the forest he wandred up and down, and at last met with a lusty tinker that had a good staff on his shoulder and a great dog to carry his bag and tools. So Tom asked the tinker from whence he came, and whither he was going, for that was no highway. But the tinker being a sturdy fellow bid him go look, and what was that to him, but fools must be meddling. No, says Tom, but I'le make you to know before you and I part it is to me. I, said the tinker, I have been these three long years and have not had one combat with any man. I have challenged many a man but none durst make me answer; I think, said he, they be all cowards in this country, but I hear there is a man in this country which is called Tom Hickathrift that killed a gyant; him I would fain see, said the tinker, to have one combat with him. I, said Tom, but methinks, said he, it might be master with you; I am the man, said he, what have you to say to me? Why verily, said the tinker, I am glad we are so happily met together, that we may have one single combat. Sure, said Tom, you do but jest. Marry, said the tinker, I am in earnest. A match, said Tom. 'Tis done, said the tinker. But, said Tom, will you give me leave to get me a twig? I, said the tinker, hang him that will fight with a man unarmed, I scorn that.

So Tom steps to the gate and takes one of the rails for his staff; so to it they fell, the Tinker at Tom, and Tom at the Tinker, like two giants they laid on at each other. The Tinker had a leathern coat on, and at every blow Tom gave the Tinker, his coat roar'd again, yet the Tinker did not give way to Tom an inch. But Tom gave the Tinker a blow on the side of the head, which felled the Tinker. Now, Tinker, where are you? said Tom.

But the Tinker being a nimble fellow, leapt up again, and gave Tom a blow, made him reel again, and followed his blows, and took Tom on the other side which made Tom's neck crack again. So Tom flung down his weapon and yielded the Tinker the better on't, and took him home to his house, where I shall leave Tom and the Tinker till they be recovered of their sad wounds and bruises.

FINIS.

THE PLEASANT HISTORY

OF

THOMAS HICKATHRIFT.

THE SECOND PART.

CHAP. I.

Tom Hickathrift and the Tinker conquered and overcame three thousand rebellious subjects.

In and about the Isle of Ely, many disaffected persons, to the number of ten thousand and upwards drew themselves up in a body, presuming to contend for their pretended ancient Rights and Liberties, insomuch that the Gentry and civil Magistrates of the Country was in great danger; at which time the Sheriff, by night, privately got into the house of Thomas Hickathrift, as a secure place of refuge, in so eminent a time of danger : where before Thomas Hickathrift, he laid open the villainous intent of this headstrong giddy-brained multitude, Mr. Sheriff, quoth Tom, what service my brother, meaning the Tinker, and I can perform, shall not be wanting. This said, in the morning by day-break, with trusty clubs they both went forth, desiring the Sheriff to be their guide, in conducting them to the place of the rebels' rendezvous, when they came there Tom and the Tinker marched up to the head of the multitude, and demanded of them the reason why they disturbed the Government? To which they answered with a loud cry, Our will's our law; and by that alone will we be governed. Nay quoth Tom if it be so, these trusty clubs are our weapons, and by them you shall be chastised. Which words were no sooner out of his mouth but the Tinker and he put themselves both together in the midst of the throng and with their clubs beat the multitude down, trampling them under their feet every blow which they struck laid twenty or thirty sprawling before them. Nay, remarkable it was, the Tinker struck a tall man just upon the nape of the neck, with that force that his head flew off, and was carried violently fourteen foot from him, where it knockt down one of their chief ringleaders; Tom on the other hand still pressing forward, till by an unfortunate blow he broke his club; yet he was not in the least dismay'd; for he presently seized upon a lusty stout rawbon'd miller, and made use of him for a weapon, till at length they clear'd the field; so that there was not one found that dare lift up a hand against them, having run into holes and corners to hide themselves shortly after some of their heads were taken and made public examples of justice, the rest being pardoned at the humble request of Thomas Hicka-thrift and the Tinker.

.

CHAP. II.

Tom Hickathrift and the Tinker was sent for to Court and of their kind entertainment there, etc.

The King being truly informed of the faithful services perform'd by these his loving Subjects, Thomas Hickathrift and the Tinker, he was pleased to send for them to his Palace, where a Royal banquet was prepared for their entertainment, most of the Nobility being present. Now after the banquet was over, the King said unto all that were there, these are my trusty and well-beloved subjects, men of approved courage and valour, they are the men that overcame and conquer'd ten thousand which were got together to disturb the peace of my realm; according to the character that hath been given to Tho. Hickathrift and Henry Nonsuch, persons here present, they cannot be matcht in any other kingdom in the world; were it possible to have an army of twenty thousand such as these, I dare venture to act the part of Alexander the Great over again: yet in the meanwhile, as a proof of my Royal favour, kneel down and receive the antient order of knighthood, Mr. Hickathrift, which was instantly perform'd. And as for Henry Nonesuch, I will settle upon him, as a reward for his great service, the sum of Forty Shillings a year, during life. Which said, the King withdrew, and Sir Thomas Hickathrift and Henry Nonesuch the tinker, returned home, attended by many persons of quality, some miles from the Court. But to the great grief of Sir Thomas, at his return from the Court, he found his aged Mother drawing to her end, who in a few days after died and was buried in the Isle of Ely.

CHAP. III.

Tom after his old Mother's death went a wooing ; and how he served a young Gallant who affronted him before his Mistress.

Tom's mother being dead, and he left alone in a large and spacious house, he found himself strange and uncouth, therefore he began to consider with himself that it would not be amiss to seek out for a wife; and hearing of a young rich widow, not far from Cambridge, to her he went, and made his addresses: and at the first coming she seem'd to shew him much favour and countenance; but between this and his coming again, she had given some entertainment to a more genteel and airy spark, who happened likewise to come while honest Tom was there the second time; he look'd wishfully at Tom, and he star'd as wishfully at him again; at last the young spark began with abuseful language to affront Tom, telling him he was such a great lubberly whelp, adding that such a one as he should not pretend to make love to a Lady, as he was but a Brewer's servant. Scoundrel quoth Tom better words should become you, and if you do not mend your manners, you shall not fail to feel my sharp correction. At which the young Spark challenged him forth into the back yard; for, as he said, he did not question but to make a fool of Tom in a trice. Into the yard they both walk together, the young spark with a naked sword, and Tom with neither stick nor staff in his hand, nor any other weapon. What says the spark, have you nothing to defend yourself? well I shall the sooner dispatch you. Which said, he ran furiously forward, making a pass at Tom, which he put by, and then wheeling round to his backside, Tom gave him such a swinging kick on the breech, which sent the spark like a Crow up into the Air, from whence he fell upon the ridge of a thatcht house, and then came down into a large fish pond, and had been certainly drown'd if it had not been for a poor shepherd who was walking that way, and seeing him float upon the water, dragged him out with his hook, and home he returned like a drowned Rat; while Tom enjoy'd the kind embraces of his fair Mistress.

CHAP. IV.

Tom served two Troopers, whom the young Spark had hired to beset him, etc.

This young galland being tormented in his mind to think how Tom had conquered and sham'd him before his Mistress, he was now resolved for speedy revenge ; and knowing that he was not able to coap with a man of Tom's strength and activity, he therefore hired two lusty Troopers, well mounted, to lie in ambush in a thicket which Tom had to pass through from his home to the young lady, and accordingly they attempted to set upon him : How now quoth Tom Rascals, what would you be at ? Are you indeed weary of the world, that you so unadvisably set upon one who is able to crush you in like a Cucumber ; the Troopers laughing at him, said, that they were not to be daunted at his high words, High words quoth Tom, no I will come to action ; and with that he run in between these armed Troopers, catching them under his arm. Horse and Men, with as much ease as if they had been but a couple of Baker's babbins, steering his course with them hastily towards his own home, and, as he pass'd thro' a meadow, in which there was many Haymakers at work, the poor distressed troopers crying out, Stop him stop him he runs away with two of the King's troopers. The hay-makers laught heartily to see how Tom hugged them along ; ever and anon he upbraided them for their baseness ; declared that he would make minced meat of them to feed the Crows and Jackdaws about his house and habitation. This was such a dreadful lecture to them, that the poor rogues begg'd that he would be merciful, and spare their lives, and they would discover the whole plot, and who was the person that employ'd them ; which accordingly they did, and gain'd favour in the sight of Tom, who pardon'd them upon promise that they would never be concern'd in such a villainous action for the time to come.

CHAP. V.

Tom going to be married, was set upon by one-and-twenty Ruffians in Armour, and of the havock he made amongst them, etc.

In regard Tom had been hinder'd by these troopers, he delay'd his visit to his Lady till next day, and then coming to her, gave her a full account of what had happen'd; she was pleased at heart at this wonderful relation, knowing it was safe for a woman to marry with a man who was able to defend her against all assaults whatsoever, and such a one she found Tom to be. The day of marriage was accordingly appointed, friends and relations invited. Yet secret malice which is never satisfied without sweet revenge, had like to have prevented the solemnity for having three miles to go to church, where they were to be married, the aforesaid Gentleman had provided a second time Ruffians in armour to the number of twenty-one, he himself being then present either to destroy the life of Tom, or put them into strange consternation; however thus it happened, in a lonesome place they bolted out upon them, making their first assault upon Tom, and with a Speer gave him a slight wound, at which his love and the rest of the women shrieked and cry'd like persons out of their wits, Tom endeavour'd all that he could to pacify them, saying, stand you still and I will show you pleasant sport. And with that he catch'd a back sword from the side of a Gentleman in his own company, with which he so bravely behaved himself that at every stroke he cut off a joint, loth he was to touch the life of any, but aiming at their legs and arms, he lopt them off so fast, that in less than a quarter of an hour, there was not one in the company but what had lost a limb, the green grass being stained with their purple gore, and the ground strew'd with legs and arms, as 'tis with tiles from the tops of the Houses after a dreadful storm. His Love and the rest of the company standing all the while as joyful spectators, laughing one at another, saying, What a company of cripples has he made, as it were in the twinkling of an eye! Yes, quoth Tom, I believe that for every drop of blood that I lost, I have made the Rascals pay me a limb as a just tribute. This done, he stept to a Farmer's hard by, and hired there a servant giving him twenty shillings to carry these cripples home to their respective habitations in his dung-cart; and then did he hasten with his love to the church, where they were married, and then returned home, where they were heartily merry with their friends, after their fierce and dreadful encounter.

CHAP. VI.

*Tom made a feast for all the poor Widows in the adjacent towns;
and how he served an old Woman who stole a Silver Cup at the
same time, etc.*

Now Tom being married, he made a plentiful feast, to which
he invited all the poor widows in four or five parishes for the
sake of his mother, which he had lately buried, this feast
was kept in his own house, with all manner of varieties that the
country could afford for the space of four days, in honour likewise
of the four victories which he lately obtain'd. Now when the
time of feasting was ended, a Silver Cup was missing, and being
ask'd about it, they every one deny'd they knew any thing of it. At
length it was agreed that they should all stand the search, which
they did, and the Cup was found upon a certain old woman,
named the Widow Stumbelow; then was all the rest in a rage,
some was for hanging her, others were for chopping the old
woman in pieces, for her ingratitude to such a generous soul as
Sir Thomas Hickathrift; but he entreated them all to be
quiet, saying they should not murder a poor old Woman, for he

would appoint a punishment for her himself; which was this; he bor'd a hole thro' her nose and tying a string therein, then order'd her to be stript stark naked, commanding the rest of the old women to stick a candle in her fundament, and lead her by the nose thro' all the streets and lanes in Cambridge, which comical sight caused a general laughter. This done, she had her cloaths restor'd her again, and so was acquitted.

F

CHAP. VII.

Sir Thomas Hickathrift and his Lady was sent for to Court, and of what happened.

The tydings of Tom's wedding was soon nois'd in the Court, so that the King sent them a royal invitation to the end he might see his Lady, they immediately went, and were received with all demonstrations of Joy and Triumph. But while they were in their mirth, a dreadful cry approached the Court which proved to be the Commons of Kent who were come thither to complain of a dreadful Giant that was landed in one of the Islands: And brought with him abundance of Bears and young Lyons, likewise a dreadful Dragon on which he himself rid, which monster and ravenous beasts had frighted all the inhabitants out of the Island. Moreover they said if speedy course was not taken to suppress them in time, they might over-run the whole land The King hearing this dreadful relation was a little startled, yet he perswaded them to return home and make the best defence they could for themselves at present, assuring them that he should not forget them, and so they departed.

CHAP. VIII.

Thomas Hickathrift was made Governor of the Island of the East Angles, now called Thanet, and of the wonderful Achievements he performed there.

The King hearing the aforesaid dreadful Tydings, immediately sate in Council to consider what was to be done for the overcoming this monstrous Giant, and barbarous savage Lyons and Bears that with him had invaded his Princely territories. At length it was agreed upon that Thomas Hickathrift was the most likeliest man in the whole kingdom, for undertaking of so dangerous an enterprise; he being not only a fortunate man of great strength, but likewise a true and trusty subject one that was always ready and willing to do his King and country service, for which reason it was thought necessary to make him Governor of the aforesaid Island; which place of trust and honour, he readily received, and accordingly he forthwith went down with his wife and family, to take possession of the same, attended with a hundred Knights and Gentlemen, who conducted him to the entrance of the Island which he was to govern. A castle in those days there was, in which he was to take up his head-quarters, the same being situated with that advantage that he could view the Island for several miles upon occasion ; the Knights and Gentlemen at last taking their leave of him, wish'd him all happy success and prosperity. Many days he had not been there before it was his fortune to behold the monstrous Giant mounted upon a dreadful Dragon, bearing upon his shoulder a club of Iron, having but one eye, the which was placed in his forehead, and larger in compass than a barber's bason, and seem'd to appear like a flaming fire ; his visage was dreadful, grim and tawny ; the hair of his head hanging down his back and shoulders, like snakes of a prodigious length ; the bristles of his beard like rusty wire :   And lifting up his blare eye, he happened to discover Sir Thomas Hickathrift, who was looking upon him from one of his windows of the castle ; the Giant then began to knit his brow, and breath forth threatening words to the Governor, who indeed was a little surpriz'd at the approach of so monstrous a brute ; the Giant finding that Tom did not make much haste down to meet him, he alighted from the back of the dragon, and chained the same to an Oak tree, then marching furiously to the castle, setting his broad shoulder against a corner of the stone walls, as if he intended to overthrow the whole building at once which Tom perceiving, said is this the game you would be at ; faith I shall spoil your sport, for I have a delicate tool to pick your teeth withal ; then taking his two handed sword of five foot long, a weapon which the King had given him to govern with taking this I say, down he went, and flinging open the Gates, he there found the Giant, who by an unfortunate slip in his thrusting was fallen all along, where he lay and could not help himself. What, quoth Tom, do you come here to take up your Lodging? This is not to be suffer'd, and with that he ran his long broad sword in betwixt the monstrous Giant's brawny Buttocks and out at his Belly, which made the monstrous Brute give such a terrible groan that it seemed like roaring thunder, making the very neighbouring trees to tremble; and then Tom pulling out his sword again, at six or seven blows he separated his head from his unconscionable trunk, which head, when it was off, seemed like the root of a mighty Oak. Then turning to the Dragon, which was all this while chain'd to a tree, without any farther discourse, with four blows with his two-handed sword, he cut off his head also. This fortunate adventure being over, he sent immediately for a team of horses and a waggon : which he loaded with these heads, and then summoning all the Constables in the Country for a guard, sent them to Court, with a promise to his Majesty, that he would rid the whole Island likewise of Bears and Lyons before he left it.

CHAP. IX.

The Tinker hearing of Tom's Fame went down to be Partner in his Enterprize; and how he was unfortunately slain by a Lyon.

Tom's victories rang so long, that they reach'd the ears of his old acquaintance, the Tinker, who, desirous of honour, resolved to go down and visit Tom in his new government, when coming there he met with kind and loving entertainment, for they were very joyful to see one another : Now after three or four days' enjoyment of one another's company, Tom told the Tinker that he must needs go forth in search after wild Bears and Lyons, in order to rout them out of the Island. Well, quoth the Tinker, I would gladly take my fortune with you, hoping that I may be serviceable to you, upon occasion. Well, quoth Tom, with all my heart, for I must needs acknowledge I shall be right glad of your company. This said, they both went forward, Tom with his two handed sword, and the Tinker with his long pike-staff. Now after they had travelled about four or five hours, it was their fortune to light of the whole knot of wild beasts together, being in number fourteen, of which six of them were Bears, the other eight young Lyons now when they had fastened their eyes upon Tom and the Tinker, these ravenous beasts began to roar and run furiously, as if they would have devoured them at a mouthful ; but Tom and the Tinker stood side by side with their backs against an Oak, and as the Lyons and Bears came within their reach, Tom with his long sword clove their heads asunder till they were all destroyed, saving one lyon, who, seeing the rest of his Fellows slain, was endeavouring to make his escape : now the Tinker being somewhat too venturous, ran too hastily after him, and having given the Lyon one blow, he turn'd upon him again, seizing him by the throat with that violence, that the poor Tinker fell dead to the Ground ; Tom Hickathrift, seeing this, gave the Lyon such a blow that it ended his life.

Now was his joy mingled with sorrow for tho' he had cleared the Island of those ravenous savage beasts, yet his grief was intolerable for the loss of his old friend. Home he returned to his lady, where in token of Joy for the wonderful success which he had in his dangerous enterprizes, he made a very noble and splendid Feast, to which he invited most of his best Friends and Acquaintance, to whom he made the following Promise.

> My Friends while I have Strength to stand,
>   most manfully I will pursue
> All Dangers, till I clear this Land,
>   of Lions, Bears, and Tygers too;
> This you'll find true, or I'm to blame,
>   let it remain upon Record;
> Tom Hickathrift's most glorious fame,
>   who never yet has broke his word

The Man who does his Country bless,
  shall merrit much from this fair land ;
He who relieved them in Distress,
  His Fame upon Record shall stand:
And you my Friends who hear me now,
  let honest Tom, for ever dwell,
Within your Minds and Thoughts I trow,
  since he has pleas'd you all so well.

FINIS.

h

www.ingramcontent.com/pod-product-compliance
Lightning Source LLC
Chambersburg PA
CBHW022029080426
42733CB00007B/777